Jonathan Edwards

JONATHAN EDWARDS
October 5, 1703 – March 22, 1758

*Prayer seemed to be natural to me,
as a breath by which the inward
burnings of my heart had vent.*

JONATHAN EDWARDS

His Doctrine of & Devotion to Prayer

Brian G. Najapfour

BIBLICAL SPIRITUALITY PRESS

Jonathan Edwards: His Doctrine of & Devotion to Prayer

Published by
Biblical Spirituality Press
6940 Hanna Lake Ave., SE
Caledonia, MI 49316
Phone: (616) 698-7467
E-mail: biblicalspiritualitypress@gmail.com
Website: biblicalspiritualitypress.org

ISBN: 978-0-9889498-0-5

First printing 2013
Second printing 2017

Printed in the United States of America

Table of Contents

In giving Jonathan Edwards to the church, God did her an inestimable favor. In giving Jonathan Edwards to the reader, Brian Najapfour has done the Christian a great favor.

Edwards rightly stands at the fountainhead of a great theological tradition. The depth of Edwards' theology, however, often overwhelms the uninitiated. In response, the reader turns to shallower streams and dies instead of theological thirst. The great riches of Edwards await those who will swim against the current. Those who persevere find not only the majesty of his thought on such great doctrines as the will and sin. They find on the far shores of their efforts the gems, ideas and doctrines directly related to God's call upon every Christian. Edwards' theology of prayer is such a gem. Given the chance, Jonathan Edwards and this volume, *Jonathan Edwards: His Doctrine of & Devotion to Prayer,* promise to change the way we pray.

—Dr. Peter Beck, Assistant Professor of Religion,
Charleston Southern University

Thomas Shepard, the Harvard man, once quipped that there are times in his life when he'd rather die than pray. No doubt we sometimes feel this way. This book on the man from Yale by Brian Najapfour will help remedy the problem of prayerlessness. For that reason alone I am grateful for this enjoyable read on the prayer life of Jonathan Edwards.

—Dr. Mark Jones, Minister of Faith Presbyterian Church (PCA),
Vancouver, British Columbia and Research Associate,
University of the Free State, Bloemfontein, South Africa

Brian Najapfour weaves together a beautiful tapestry of theology and piety, of doctrine and devotion, from the life, sermons and writings of Jonathan Edwards. You'll end up knowing much more about this godly man; but, if you follow his example, you'll end up knowing even more about God.

—Dr. David P. Murray, Professor of Old Testament and Practical
Theology, Puritan Reformed Theological Seminary

Historically informed and contemporarily relevant, *Jonathan Edwards: His Doctrine of & Devotion to Prayer* equips one in the life of prayer.

—Dr. Adriaan C. Neele, Associate Editor and Director of the
Jonathan Edwards Center, Yale University Divinity School

To my godly and generous parents-in-law
Rev. Bartel and Mrs. Joan Elshout,
the best in-laws on earth

Foreword

If you're a Christian, you know that nothing can produce guilt in you so quickly as when a preacher tells you what your prayer life ought to be like. How far short we all fall in terms of the ideal prayer life! And yet, it is good to hear about how we should be praying—not to stir up guilt so much as to arouse our too lukewarm spirits to get back on our knees to praise, thank, and cry out to the glorious God of our salvation.

I can scarcely think of a better theologian and preacher to stir us up to prayer than Jonathan Edwards (1703–1758). His scripturalness, glorious focus on the Trinity, and personal wrestlings (life-long!) in prayer and for prayer make him an ideal study on prayer. This short book on Edwards' doctrine of and devotion to prayer is just what we need to arouse our naturally lazy souls and minds to better and more earnest prayer; it will not disappoint you. Here you will find spiritual instruction, nourishment, encouragement, insight, and challenge.

Brian Najapfour winsomely shows us how Edwards' optimism about prayer, both privately and unitedly, ought to move us to prioritize prayer in our lives. In prayer we commune with the Father and the Son by the Spirit more intimately than through any other means of grace. What a blessing prayer is to a Christian! Let these pages serve as a tonic for our weak prayers and as an inspiration to beg of the Holy Spirit to awaken us to a more real and fervent life of communion with the triune God.

—Joel R. Beeke

Acknowledgments

I want to thank Dr. Michael A. G. Haykin for his wise suggestions to improve the manuscript. Thanks also to Dr. Joel R. Beeke for his gracious foreword, to Beth Bouman and Gary den Hollander for their proofreading help, to Gina Bessetti-Reyes for her editing expertise, to Linda den Hollander for her beautiful typesetting, and to Amy Zevenbergen for the attractive cover design.

My gratitude also goes to my dear wife Sarah, my faithful prayer partner, encourager, and editor.

Above all, I am thankful to God for the gift of prayer through which I can commune with Him anytime and anywhere. Oh, what a great privilege to pray to Him!

INTRODUCTION

———— ✦ ————

Jonathan Edwards:

His Doctrine of and Devotion to Prayer

*Personal communion with the Almighty, which
was to be a hallmark of his theology, was an
experience Edwards sought on a daily basis.*
—George S. Claghorn

In his book, *A Sweet Flame: Piety in the Letters of
Jonathan Edwards*, published in 2007, the noted
church historian Michael Haykin observes, "In the
past forty years the books, essays, and doctoral the-
ses on Jonathan Edwards' theology have become
a veritable flood. Yet there still remains much to
be done regarding various details of his piety. For
example, there still needs to be written a major
study on Edwards' theology of prayer."[1] The purpose of this booklet then is to contribute to that need
by providing an overview of Edwards' teachings on

---

1. Michael A. G. Haykin, *A Sweet Flame: Piety in the Letters of
Jonathan Edwards* (Grand Rapids: Reformation Heritage Books,
2007), 167.

and practice of prayer.[2] In the following pages, I
will sketch Edwards' prayer life, his description of
and devotion to prayer, his doctrine of prayer, and
his distinct emphasis on the Holy Spirit in prayer.
In conclusion, some practical lessons will be derived
from Edwards' prayer life.

---

2. Some scholars have begun exploring this topic. For instance,
see Robert Oscar Bakke's "The Concert of Prayer: Back to the
Future?" (D.Min. diss., Gordon-Conwell Theological Seminary,
1993). However, while Bakke discusses Edwards' teachings
on prayer, he only focuses on Edwards' treatise known as *An
Humble Attempt.* Likewise, Glenn R. Kreider's article, "Jonathan
Edwards's Theology of Prayer," *Bibliotheca Sacra* 160 (2003),
examines Edwards' theology of prayer, but only in conjunction
with his sermon, *The Most High, A Prayer-Hearing God.* Most
recently Peter Beck wrote "The Voice of Faith: Jonathan Edwards's
Theology of Prayer" (Ph.D. diss., Southern Baptist Theological
Seminary, 2007), a study published in 2010 by Joshua Press. In my
opinion, Beck's work meets the need that Haykin has mentioned.
Given the lengthy nature of Beck's volume, I have decided to
publish my booklet that will provide the reader with a summary of
Edwards' doctrine of and devotion to prayer.

CHAPTER ONE

———— ✦ ————

Dawn of His Prayer Life

Born on October 5, 1703, in East Windsor, Connecticut, Jonathan Edwards, often considered to be
the last Puritan,[1] is widely regarded as the greatest theologian of his time. Despite this distinction,
few people recognize him as a great man of prayer.
Peter Beck, in his doctoral dissertation on Edwards'
theology of prayer, rightly calls Edwards "the theologian of prayer."[2] What follows is a cursory look at
Edwards' prayer life.

Brought up in a Christian home, as the only boy
among eleven children, Edwards lived in a prayerful atmosphere. Edwards' great-grandson, Sereno
Dwight (1786–1850) points out that both Edwards'
parents (his father, Timothy, who was a minister,

---

1. See David C. Brand, *Profile of the Last Puritan: Jonathan
Edwards, Self-Love, and the Dawn of the Beatific* (Atlanta, Ga.:
Scholars Press, 1991).

2. Peter Beck, "The Voice of Faith: Jonathan Edwards's Theology of Prayer" (Ph.D. diss., Southern Baptist Theological Seminary, 2007), 300.

and his mother, Esther, who was a godly woman) reared him with prayers:

> Many were the prayers presented by parental affection that this only and beloved son might be filled with the Holy Spirit; from a child know the Holy Scriptures; and be great in the sight of the Lord. They who thus fervently and constantly commended him to God, manifested equal diligence in training him up for God. Prayer excited to exertion, and exertion again was encouraged by prayer. The domestic circle was a scene of supplication, and it was a scene of instruction.
>
> The faithful religious instructions of his parents "rendered him when a child familiarly conversant with God and Christ, with his own character and duty, with the way of salvation, and with the nature of that eternal life which, begun on earth, is perfected in heaven." *Their prayers were not forgotten, and their efforts did not remain without effect.*[3]

Reading Dwight's account explains why Edwards, as young as seven or eight years old, already prayed with what may be labeled extraordinary zeal. Recalling his childhood, Edwards, when he was about thirty-five years old, records his impressions in his *Personal Narrative*:[4]

---

3. Sereno E. Dwight, "Memoirs of Jonathan Edwards," in *The Works of Jonathan Edwards*, vol. 1, ed. Edward Hickman (1834; reprint, Edinburgh: Banner of Truth Trust, 1974), xii (italics mine).

4. See Donald S. Whitney, "Pursuing A Passion For God Through Spiritual Disciplines: Learning From Jonathan Edwards," in *A*

I had a variety of concerns and exercises about my soul from my childhood; but I had two more remarkable seasons of awakening, before I met with that change by which I was brought to those new dispositions, and that new sense of things, that I have since had, the first time was when I was a boy, some years before I went to college, at a time of remarkable awakening in my father's congregation. I was then very much affected for many months, and concerned about the things of religion, and my soul's salvation; and was abundant in religious duties. *I used to pray five times a day in secret and to spend much time in religious conversation with other boys; and used to meet with them to pray together.*[5]

Edwards adds an illustration of how his delight in the Lord impacted his activities:

I experienced I know not what kind of delight in religion. My mind was much engaged in it, and had much self-righteous pleasure, and it was my delight to abound in religious duties. *I, with some of my schoolmates, joined together and built a booth in a swamp, in a very retired spot, for a place of prayer. And besides, I had particular secret places of my own in the woods, where I used to retire by myself; and was from time to time much affected.*[6]

God Entranced Vision of All Things: The Legacy of Jonathan Edwards, eds. John Piper and Justin Taylor (Wheaton: Crossway Books, 2004), 117.

5. Cited in Dwight, "Memoirs of Jonathan Edwards," xii (italics mine).

6. Ibid., (italics mine).

The very young Edwards already showed maturity in his prayer life. But, as Haykin recognizes, "[T]his childhood spirituality—albeit a prognostication of his future interests—soon disappeared."[7] The time came that the young Edwards completely lost his zeal in prayer:

> But, in progress of time, my convictions and affections wore off, and I entirely lost all those affections and delights, and left off secret prayer, at least as to any constant preference of it; and turned like a dog to his vomit, and went on in the ways of sin. Indeed, I was at times very uneasy, especially towards the latter part of my time at college, when it pleased God to seize me with a pleurisy; in which he brought me nigh to the grave and shook me over the pit of hell. And yet it was not long after my recovery, before I fell again into my old ways of sin.[8]

At this time, Edwards was actually struggling with the experience of salvation:

> My concern now wrought more by inward struggles and conflicts, and self-reflection. I made seeking my salvation the main business of my life. But yet, it seems to me, I sought it after a miserable manner which has made me sometimes since to question, whether ever it issued in that which was saving; being ready

---

7. Michael A. G. Haykin, *Jonathan Edwards: The Holy Spirit in Revival* (Darlington, Co. Durham/Webster, NY: Evangelical Press, 2005), 8.

8. Cited in Dwight, "Memoirs of Jonathan Edwards," xii.

to doubt whether such miserable seeking ever succeeded. I was indeed brought to seek salvation, in a manner that I never was before; I felt a spirit to part with all things in the world, for an interest in Christ. My concern continued, and prevailed, with many exercising thoughts and inward struggles; but yet it never seemed to be proper, to express that concern by the name of terror.[9]

One of Edwards' struggles was about the doctrine of God's sovereignty in connection to salvation. He could not accept this doctrine because it appeared "like a horrible doctrine" to him.[10] However, when he, through the "extraordinary influence of God's Spirit," became "convinced, and fully satisfied" with this doctrine, his mind began to rest in it.[11] What he previously called "a horrible doctrine" now became "pleasant, bright, and sweet" for him.[12] This experience, coupled with his encounter with the words in 1 Timothy 1:17: "Now unto the King eternal, immortal, invisible, the only wise God, be honour and glory for ever and ever. Amen,"[13] brought him a "sort of

9. Ibid.
10. Ibid.
11. Ibid.
12. Ibid., xiii.
13. All scriptural quotations in this paper are directly taken from Edwards' pen, unless noted otherwise. In this regard, two things should be remembered: (1) Edwards consistently used the 1611 King James Version of the Bible in his sermons, and (2) as John F. Wilson observes, "Edwards appears to have quoted Scripture from memory, and he is not always accurate." Cited

inward, sweet delight in God and divine things."[14] As Edwards writes:

> As I read the words [in 1 Timothy 1:17], there came into my soul, and was as it were diffused through it, a sense of the glory of the Divine Being; a new sense, quite different from any thing I ever experienced before. Never any words of Scripture seemed to me as these words did. I thought with myself, how excellent a Being that was, and how happy I should be, if I might enjoy that God, and be rapt up to him in heaven; and be as it were swallowed up in him for ever![15]

He continues, describing the new aspects of his prayer life:

> I kept saying, and as it were singing, over these words of Scripture to myself; *and went to pray to God that I might enjoy him; and prayed in a manner quite different from what I used to do, with a new sort of affection.* But it never came into my thought, that there was any thing spiritual, or of a saving nature, in this.[16]

The glorious experience described above marks Edwards' conversion in 1721, which probably occurred during the spring[17] of his seventeenth

---

in Glenn R. Kreider, "Jonathan Edwards's Theology of Prayer," *Bibliotheca Sacra* 160 (2003), 437.

14. Cited in Dwight, "Memoirs of Jonathan Edwards," xiii.

15. Ibid.

16. Ibid., (italics mine).

17. Haykin, *Jonathan Edwards: The Holy Spirit in Revival*, 8. Whitney also holds the same date (spring of 1721), "Pursuing A Passion For God Through Spiritual Disciplines: Learning From

year.[18] With great joy Edwards further shares his experience of salvation:

> From about that time I began to have a new kind of apprehensions and ideas of Christ, and the work of redemption, and the glorious way of salvation by him. An inward, sweet sense of these things, at times, came into my heart; and my soul was led away in pleasant views and contemplation of them. And my mind was greatly engaged to spend time in reading and meditating on Christ, on the beauty and excellency of his person, and the lovely way of salvation by free grace in him.[19]

What is noteworthy here is Edwards' testimony that after his conversion he prayed quite differently than he used to. He now prayed with an affection that he describes as novel or previously unfelt. This change in his prayer life indicates that he only truly enjoyed communing with God after knowing the Lord Jesus

Jonathan Edwards," 112. For more details about the date of Edwards' conversion, see Iain H. Murray, *Jonathan Edwards: A New Biography* (Edinburg: Banner of Truth Trust, 1996), 35–37. See also George M. Marsden, *Jonathan Edwards: A Life* (New Haven: Yale University Press, 2003), 39–43. I owe these references to Haykin in his endnotes, *Jonathan Edwards: The Holy Spirit in Revival*, 186. One may also want to see the first chapter of Harold Simonson's book chapter-titled "Edwards' Record of Conversion," found in *Jonathan Edwards: Theologian of the Heart*, (Grand Rapids: Eerdmans Publishing Company, 1974), 17–32.

18. Edwards was born October 5, 1703. Thus, assuming his conversion took place during the spring of 1721, he was then seventeen years old.

19. Cited in Dwight, "Memoirs of Jonathan Edwards," xiii.

Christ savingly. Edwards' childhood prayer life was not an activity of his born-again soul but rather a manifestation of God's common grace in his life. Edwards depicts his pre-conversion prayer life as superficial: "Those former delights never reached the heart; and did not arise from any sight of the divine excellency of the things of God; or any taste of the soul-satisfying and life giving good there is in them."[20]

In light of Edwards' account of his prayer life, two important points can be observed. First, even an unbeliever can have zeal in prayer, but without genuine conversion, this zeal will eventually expire; and second, only when one experiences authentic conversion can that person really come with delight and passion to God in prayer.

---

20. Ibid.

CHAPTER TWO

———— ✦ ————

Description of Prayer and His Devotion to It

A. Customary Work of the Soul

Edwards understands prayer as a natural work of the born-again soul. Writing of the transformation in his life, Edwards says:

> My mind was greatly fixed on divine things; almost perpetually in the contemplation of them. I spent most of my time in thinking of divine things, year after year; often walking alone in the woods, and solitary places, for meditation, soliloquy, and prayer, and converse with God; and it was always my manner, at such times, to sing forth my contemplations. I was almost constantly in ejaculatory prayer, wherever I was.[1]

Then here comes his famous line in prayer: "Prayer seemed to be natural to me, as a breath by which the inward burnings of my heart had vent."[2] George

---

1. Cited in Sereno E. Dwight, "Memoirs of Jonathan Edwards," in *The Works of Jonathan Edwards*, vol. 1, ed. Edward Hickman (1834; reprint, Edinburgh: Banner of Truth Trust, 1974), xiii.
2. Ibid.

Marsden, who has written a massive biography of Edwards, succinctly summarizes Edwards' prayer life. This summary displays how natural or customary prayer was to Edwards:

> Edwards usually rose at four or five in the morning in order to spend thirteen hours in his study.... He began the day with private prayers followed by family prayers, by candlelight in winter. Each meal was accompanied by household devotions, and at the end of each day Sarah [his wife] joined him in his study for prayers. Jonathan kept secret the rest of his daily devotional routine, following Jesus' command to pray in secret. Throughout the day, his goal was to remain constantly with a sense of living in the presence of God, as difficult as that might be. Often he added secret days of fasting and additional prayers.[3]

Donald Whitney adds, "Prayer, then, for Edwards was both planned and informal, scheduled and spontaneous, on a daily basis."[4] Indeed, on the day Edwards was saved, prayers began to flow naturally from his new life. Edwards would agree with his fellow Puritan William Gurnall (1617–1679): "[Prayer

---

3. George M. Marsden, *Jonathan Edward: A Life* (New Haven: Yale University Press, 2003), 133.

4. Donald S. Whitney, "Pursuing A Passion For God Through Spiritual Disciplines: Learning From Jonathan Edwards," in *A God Entranced Vision of All Things: The Legacy of Jonathan Edwards*, eds. John Piper and Justin Taylor (Wheaton: Crossway Books, 2004), 115.

is] the same to the new creature as crying is to the natural. The child is not learned by art or example to cry, but instructed by nature; it comes into the world crying. Praying is not a lesson got by forms and rules of art, but flowing from principles of new life."[5]

B. Closet Prayer

Closet or secret prayer for Edwards was of great importance. Samuel Hopkins is able to testify of this:

> Mr. Edwards made a secret of his private devotion, and therefore it cannot be particularly known: though there is much evidence, that he was punctual, constant and frequent in secret, and often kept days of fasting and prayer in secret; and set apart time for serious, devout meditation on spiritual and eternal things, as part of his religious exercise in secret.[6]

Normally Edwards would spend his private devotion praying for the advancement of Christ's kingdom in the world, a theme crucial to his theology: "I had great longings for the advancement of Christ's kingdom in the world; my secret prayers used to be, in great part, taken up in praying for it."[7]

Sadly, Edwards' emphasis on personal devotion

---

5. Cited in Isaac David Ellis Thomas, comp. ed., *The Golden Treasury of Puritan Quotations* (Carlisle, Pa.: Banner of Truth Trust, 1977), 209–10.

6. Cited in Whitney, "Pursuing A Passion For God Through Spiritual Disciplines: Learning From Jonathan Edwards," 119.

7. Cited in Dwight, "Memoirs of Jonathan Edwards," xiv.

often led others to accuse him of being antisocial.[8] However, Whitney explains, "Some of his habits for seclusion are understandable when we realize that his study, writing, and sermon preparation had to be done in the same house with a wife, eleven children, servants, and frequent guests."[9]

Sometimes Edwards would also go out with his friend John Smith to a solitary place to talk about the things of God:

> I very frequently used to retire into a solitary place, on the banks of Hudson's river, at some distance from the city, for contemplation on divine things and secret converse with God; and had many sweet hours there. *Sometimes Mr. Smith and I walked there together, to converse on the things of God; and our conversation used to turn much on the advancement of Christ's kingdom in the world, and the glorious things that God would accomplish for his church in the latter days.*[10]

This account shows that Edwards was not antisocial, though he tended to stress private devotion, or what he called "close meditation" or "secret converse with God." For instance, in his treatise, *On Religious Affections* (1746), he tells his readers:

Some are greatly affected when in company;

---

8. Whitney, "Pursuing A Passion For God Through Spiritual Disciplines: Learning From Jonathan Edwards," 117.

9. Ibid.

10. Cited in Dwight, "Memoirs of Jonathan Edwards," xiv (italics mine).

but have nothing that bears any manner of proportion to it in secret, in close meditation, prayer and conversing with God when alone, and separated from all the world. A true Christian doubtless delights in religious fellowship and Christian conversation, and finds much to affect his heart in it; but he also delights at times to retire from all mankind, to converse with God in solitude. And this also has its peculiar advantages for fixing his heart, and engaging his affections. True religion disposes persons to be much alone in solitary places, for holy meditation and prayer.[11]

But again his special emphasis on the practice of personal communion does not mean that he disregards the importance of public devotion:

[T]here is much in christian conversation, social and public worship, tending greatly to refresh and rejoice the hearts of the saints. But this is all that I aim at by what has been said, to show that it is the nature of true grace, however *it loves christian society in its place*, in a peculiar manner to delight in retirement, and secret converse with God.[12]

Here Edwards actually seeks to balance the vitality of private and public prayer, though as previously men-

---

11. Jonathan Edwards, "On Religious Affections," in *The Works of Jonathan Edwards*, vol. 1, ed. Edward Hickman (1834; reprint, Edinburgh: Banner of Truth Trust, 1974), 311–12. I owe this reference to Whitney, "Pursuing A Passion For God Through Spiritual Disciplines: Learning From Jonathan Edwards," 117–18.

12. Edwards, "On Religious Affections," 312 (italics his).

tioned, undeniably he gave more importance to the former. Nevertheless, for him true religion delights in both: "So that if persons appear greatly engaged in social religion, and but little in the religion of the closet, and are often highly affected when with others, and but little moved when they have none but God and Christ to converse with, it looks very darkly upon their religion."[13]

C. Concerted Prayer

In his treatise published in 1748 and titled heavily, *An Humble Attempt to Promote Explicit Agreement and Visible Union of God's People in Extraordinary Prayer, for the Revival of Religion and Advancement of Christ's Kingdom on Earth* (hereafter *An Humble Attempt*), Edwards highlights what he termed "concert for prayer," which is the opposite concept of the closet prayer. As indicated in the title of this work, Edwards is entreating God's people to unite together in not just prayer but "extraordinary prayer" that will result in the revival of religion and in the advancement of Christ's kingdom on earth.

In his introductory notes, David Bryant explains at least two reasons that Edwards wrote this treatise. "In truth," says Bryant, "*An Humble Attempt* was composed because, after two remarkable movements of God in revival ['(1) on a more local community level from 1734–35, and then (2) in the First Great

---

13. Ibid.

Awakening in the colonies, especially during the early 1740's], Edwards sensed the spiritual momentum was waning."[14] Because Edwards was so convinced that God would not send revival again until His people earnestly prayed together, he called for a concert of prayer. Glen Kreider articulates this point as follows, "Although he [Edwards] was convinced that the revival or renewal of true religion was a surprising, supernatural work of the Holy Spirit, Edwards believed that God might send a new manifestation of His Spirit in response to the prayers of His people."[15] "This conviction," writes Kreider, "is clearly stated in [Edwards'] 'Some Thoughts concerning the Revival,' written in 1742 during the revivals later known as the Great Awakening:"[16]

> It is Gods' will, through his wonderful grace, that the prayers of his saints should be one great and principal means of carrying on the designs of Christ's kingdom on earth. When God has something very great to accomplish for

---

14. David Bryant, Introduction to *A Call to United, Extraordinary Prayer...*, by Jonathan Edwards (Ross-shire, U.K.: Christian Heritage, 2003), 15–16. See also John H. Armstrong, Introduction to *Praying Together for True Revival* by Jonathan Edwards, ed. T. M. Moore (Phillipsburg, NJ: Presbyterian & Reformed Publishing, 2004), 1–10. For a more detailed introductory remark to *An Humble Attempt*, see Bakke, "The Concert of Prayer: Back to the Future?"

15. Glenn R. Kreider, "Jonathan Edwards's Theology of Prayer," *Bibliotheca Sacra* 160 (2003), 435.

16. Ibid.

his church, 'tis his will that there should pre-
cede it the extraordinary prayers of his people.[17]

Bryant also argues that Edwards wrote *An Humble Attempt* because Edwards wanted to provide
additional theological help for a document dubbed
Memorial, which was written by Scottish pastors.[18]
To explicate this so-called *Memorial*, Bryant tells a
helpful story:

> Rising out of scores of prayer societies already
> functioning in Scotland around 1740, especially
> among young people, by 1744 a committee of
> ministers determined it was time to do more.
> They decided to try a two-year 'experiment',
> uniting all prayer groups and praying Christians
> in their nation into a common prayer strategy.
> They called for focused revival prayer on every
> Saturday evening and Sunday morning, as well
> as on the first Tuesday of each quarter. By 1746
> they were so gratified by the impact of their
> experiment that they composed a call to prayer
> to the church worldwide, especially in the colo-
> nies (Memorial).[19]

Beauty of this concerted prayer. Within *An
Humble Attempt*, Edwards mentions that this orches-
trated prayer is the most beautiful and amiable
spiritual discipline that one can imagine on earth:

---

17. Cited in Ibid., 436.
18. Bryant, Introduction to *A Call to United, Extraordinary
Prayer*, 17.
19. Ibid., 16–17.

"How *condecent*, how *beautiful*, and of *good tenderly* would it be, for multitudes of Christians, in a various parts of the world, by *explicit agreement*, to unite in such prayer as is proposed to us. *Union* is one of the most *amiable* things that pertains to human society; yea, it is one of the most beautiful and happy things on earth, which indeed makes earth most like heaven."[20]

Benefit of this concerted prayer. This corporate prayer is not only beautiful, but also beneficial; as Edwards puts forth, "Such an union in prayer for the general outpouring of the Spirit of God, would not only be beautiful, but *profitable* too."[21] Then Edwards lists some benefits of this synchronized prayer:

> It would tend very much to promote union and charity between distant members of the church of Christ, to promote public spirit, love to the church of God, and concern for the interest of *Zion*; as well as be an amiable exercise and manifestation of such a spirit. Union in religious duties, especially in the duty of prayer, in praying one with and for another, and jointly for their common welfare, above almost all

---

20. Jonathan Edwards, "An Humble Attempt to Promote Explicit Agreement and Visible Union of God's People in Extraordinary Prayer, for the Revival of Religion and Advancement of Christ's Kingdom on Earth," in *The Works of Jonathan Edwards*, vol. 2, ed. Edward Hickman (1834; reprint, Edinburgh: Banner of Truth Trust, 1974), 295 (italics his).

21. Ibid., (italics his).

other things, tends to promote mutual affection and endearment.[22]

For ministers, adds Edwards, this concert of prayer,

would naturally tend to engage...[them]—the business of whose lives it should be, to seek the welfare of the church of Christ, and advancement of his kingdom—to greater diligence and earnestness in their work; and it would have a tendency to the spiritual profit and advantage of each particular person. For persons to be thus engaged in extraordinary prayer for the revival and flourishing state of religion in the world, will naturally lead each one to reflect on *himself*, and consider how religion flourishes in his own heart, and how far his example contributes to that for which he is praying.[23]

Hence we see that Edwards, as a great man of prayer, was both a private and public person. He savored both secret and social prayer in his life.

D. Connection between Prayer and Study

Another fascinating thought on prayer that Edwards had is the intermingling of prayer and study. As he was studying—approximately thirteen hours a day—he was doing so prayerfully, so that prayer and study intertwined with each other. Iain Murray, in his masterful biography of Edwards, illustrates this point well:

22. Ibid., (italics his).
23. Ibid., (italics his).

Edwards maintained daily set times for prayer, when it was probably his custom to speak aloud. He also had, as already noted, particular days which he set aside for solitude, meditation and fasting. But prayer was not a compartment in his daily routine, an exercise which possessed little connection with the remainder of his hours alone. Rather *he sought to make his study itself a sanctuary, and whether wrestling with Scripture, preparing sermons or writing in his notebooks, he worked as a worshipper. Thought, prayer and writing were all woven together.*[24]

Whitney's observation is similar: "Edwards was so devoted to prayer that it is hard to find a daily routine for him that wasn't permeated with it.... He prayed over his studies, and he prayed as he walked in the evening. Prayer was both a discipline and a part of his leisure."[25]

Even Edwards' physical exercise was permeated with prayer. Many people comment that one of Edwards' weaknesses was that he was a workaholic at the cost of his health. While this comment has an element of truth, he was not altogether neglectful of his health. In fact, in the twentieth of his *Resolutions*, written when he was nineteen years old, his concern pertains to his physical health: "Resolved,

---

24. Murray, *Jonathan Edwards: A New Biography*, 143 (italics mine).

25. Whitney, "Pursuing A Passion For God Through Spiritual Disciplines: Learning From Jonathan Edwards," 114.

to maintain the strictest temperance in eating and drinking."[26] Moreover, he himself makes a record in his *Personal Narrative* that he would ride out into woods for his health: "I rode out into the woods for my health...having alighted from my horse in a retired place, as my manner commonly has been, to walk for divine contemplation and prayer."[27] What is noteworthy here is that even his physical exercise was interfused with a spirit of prayer.

So far we have looked at some of Edwards' basic descriptions of prayer—customary, closet, and concerted—and how he himself lived out such concepts of prayer. One must remember, though, that Edwards did not just formulate these concepts from theories; rather, these concepts were based on certain doctrines that Edwards deduced from the Scriptures. As Stephen Nichols asserts, "Edwards anchors his thoughts on prayer in good theology."[28] Edwards' practice of prayer is rooted in his theology of prayer. In the following pages, we will consider Edwards' doctrine of prayer.

---

26. Jonathan Edwards, "Resolutions," in *Letters and Personal Writings*, ed. George S. Claghorn, vol. 16 of *The Works of Jonathan Edwards*, ed. Harry S. Stout (New Haven: Yale University Press, 1998), 754.

27. Cited in Whitney, "Pursuing A Passion For God Through Spiritual Disciplines: Learning From Jonathan Edwards," 117.

28. Stephen Nichols, *Jonathan Edwards: A Guided Tour of His Life and Thoughts* (Philipsburg: Presbyterian & Reformed Publishing, 2001), 206.

CHAPTER THREE

———— ✦ ————

Doctrine of Prayer

Edwards did not draw up a systematic theology; thus, much of what we know about his theology comes from his scattered writings. In the case of his doctrinal position on prayer, we have his sermons as our primary source. Prayer was one of Edwards' favorite subjects in preaching. In this section we shall look at one of Edwards' sermons, *The Most High, A Prayer-Hearing God* (1736).[1] According to Kreider this message is where "Edwards's most concise public presentation of his theology of prayer is found."[2]

Delivered on a day appointed for fasting, *The Most High, A Prayer-Hearing God* is one of Edwards' early and important sermons on prayer. He preached this sermon because of a certain epidemic that brought sickness and eventually death to his congregation. Relatives of the dead prayed,

1. Jonathan Edwards, "The Most High, A Prayer-Hearing God," in *The Works of Jonathan Edwards*, vol. 2, ed. Edward Hickman (1834; reprint, Edinburgh: Banner of Truth Trust, 1974), 113–18.

2. Glenn R. Kreider, "Jonathan Edwards's Theology of Prayer," *Bibliotheca Sacra* 160 (2003), 437.

but they felt God had not listened to them. Consequently, they started to doubt if God hears prayer.[3]
In this context Edwards preached this message. As
his sermon's title shows, he was convinced that God
is a prayer-hearing God. Edwards arrived at such
a conviction on the basis of his observation of the
words in Psalm 65:2: "O thou that hearest prayer."
Having briefly expounded this verse, Edwards concludes, "Hence we gather this doctrine, [t]hat it is
the character of the Most High, that he is a God who
hears prayer."[4] (It can be noticed from Edwards' sermons that he typically begins with a short exposition
of a text, or a verse or portion of a verse,[5] then draws
a doctrine from his exposition, and concludes with
an application or use of this doctrine.)

The substance of this sermon is well summarized
by the first paragraph of the sermon's body:

> The Most High is a God that hears prayer.
> Though he is infinitely above all, and stands
> in no need of creatures; yet he is graciously
> pleased to take a merciful notice of poor worms
> of the dust. He manifests and presents him-
> self as the object of prayer, appears as sitting
> on a mercy-seat, that men may come to him by
> prayer. When they stand in need of anything, he

---

3. Stephen Nichols, *Jonathan Edwards: A Guided Tour of His Life and Thoughts* (Philipsburg: Presbyterian & Reformed Publishing, 2001), 205–206.

4. Edwards, "The Most High, A Prayer-Hearing God," 113.

5. As in the case of *The Most High, A Prayer-Hearing God*, where Edwards only spells out the first half of the verse.

allows them to come, and ask it of him; and he is wont [i.e., accustomed] to hear their prayers. God in his word hath given many promises that he will hear their prayers; the Scripture is full of such examples; and in his dispensations towards his church, manifests himself to be a God that hears prayer.[6]

A. Doctrine Defined

As stated before, from Psalm 65:2 Edwards develops the doctrine that God is a prayer-hearing God. By this teaching Edwards means two things. First, God accepts "the supplication of those who pray to him."[7] Edwards further explains, "Their address to him is well taken, he is well pleased with it. He approves of their asking such mercies as they request of him, and approves of their manner of doing it. He accepts of their prayers as an offering to him: he accepts the honour they do him in prayer."[8]

The second meaning is that God "*acts* agreeably to his acceptance. He sometimes manifests his acceptance of their prayers by special discoveries of his mercy and sufficiency, which he makes to them *in prayer*, or immediately after. While they are praying, he gives them sweet views of his glorious grace, purity, sufficiency, and sovereignty; and enables them, with great quietness, to rest in him, to leave

---

6. Edwards, "The Most High, A Prayer-Hearing God," 114.
7. Ibid.
8. Ibid.

themselves and their prayers with him, submitting to his will, and trusting in his grace and faithfulness."[9]

Then, to avoid misunderstanding, Edwards clarifies this doctrine further:

> Not that I conclude persons can hence argue, that the particular thing which they ask will certainly be given them, or that they can particularly foretell from it what God will do in answer to their prayers, any further than he has promised in his word; yet God may, and doubtless does, thus testify his acceptance of their prayers, and from hence they may confidently rest in his providence, in his merciful ordering and disposing, with respect to the thing which they ask.[10]

B. Doctrine Displayed

Having defined this doctrine, Edwards proceeds to display it. He gives at least five areas in which this doctrine is evident.

First, through prayer God gives us *"free access"* to His throne of grace.[11] "God in his word," states Edwards, "manifests himself ready at all times to allow us this privilege [of coming to His throne of grace]. He sits on a throne of grace; and there is no veil to hide this throne, and keep us from it. The veil is rent from the top to the bottom; the way is open at all times, and we may go to God as often as we

---

9. Ibid, (italics his).
10. Ibid.
11. Ibid., (italics his).

please."[12] Then Edwards exclaims, "How wonderful is it that such worms as we should be allowed to come boldly at all times to so great a God!"[13]

Second, God hears our prayer "*so readily.*"[14] Though not always, God "often manifests his readiness to hear prayer, by giving an answer so speedily, sometimes while [we] are yet speaking, and sometimes before [we] pray." Edwards also notes that if "God defers for the present to answer the prayer of faith, it is not from any backwardness to answer, but for the good of his people sometimes, that they may be better prepared for the mercy before they receive it, or because another time would be the best and fittest on some other account."[15]

Third, God gives us "*so liberally* [i.e., generously] in answer to prayer."[16] Citing James 1:5–6, Edwards attests that "God both gives liberally, and upbraids us not with our undeservings,"[17] and that "[s]ometimes, God not only gives the thing asked, but he gives [us] more than is asked. So he did to Solomon."[18]

Fourth, God often does great things in answer to our prayer.[19] As Edwards unfolds this fourth point, he demonstrates his impressive familiarity with

---

12. Ibid.
13. Ibid.
14. Ibid., (italics his).
15. Ibid.
16. Ibid., (italics his).
17. Ibid.
18. Ibid.
19. Ibid., 115 (italics his).

the Bible, for he explains this point articulately by excerpting and integrating biblical narratives. John Gerstner is thus correct to suggest that "Edwards' reputation may be enhanced by his intimate familiarity with and constant interweaving of the sacred text in its most eloquent translation, the King James Version."[20] A reading of Edwards' explanation of God's greatness in answer to prayer will prove Gerstner's claim:

> Thus, when Esau was coming out against his brother Jacob, with four hundred men, without doubt fully resolved to cut him off, Jacob prayed and God turned the heart of Esau, so that he met Jacob in a very friendly manner; Gen. xxxii. So in Egypt, at the prayer of Moses, God brought those dreadful plagues, and at his prayer removed them again.... Joshua prayed to God, and said, "Sun, stand thou still upon Gibeon, and thou, Moon, in the valley of Ajalon;" and God heard his prayer, and caused the sun and moon to stand still accordingly.[21]

Finally, "God, as it were, [is] *overcome* by our prayer."[22] When God's people pray and God hears them, it is as if he is overcome by their prayer. Prayer "has a great power in it; such a prayer-hearing God is the Most High, that he graciously manifests himself

20. Cited in Kreider, "Jonathan Edwards's Theology of Prayer," 437.
21. Edwards, "The Most High, A Prayer-Hearing God," 115.
22. Ibid., 115 (italics his).

as conquered by it."[23] For instance, explains Edwards, when God's "anger was provoked against Israel, and he appeared to be ready to consume them in his hot displeasure, Moses stood in the gap, and by his humble and earnest prayer and supplication averted the stroke of divine vengeance."[24]

C. Doctrine Distinguished

After defining and displaying the doctrine that God is a prayer-hearing Lord, Edwards distinguishes it from doctrines of other religions whose gods are false, and therefore cannot hear prayer. Edwards opens this section by saying, "Herein the most high God is *distinguished* from false gods. The true God is the only one of this character; there is no other of whom it may be said, that he *heareth prayer*."[25] Then the last Puritan proceeds to argue:

> Many of those things that are worshipped as gods are *idols* made by their worshippers; mere stocks and stones that know nothing. They are indeed made with ears; but they hear not the prayers of them that cry to them.... Others, though not the works of men's hands, yet are things *without life*. Thus, many worship the sun, moon, and stars, which, though glorious creatures, yet are not capable of knowing any thing of the wants and desires of those who pray to them. Some worship certain kinds of animals,

---

23. Ibid.
24. Ibid.
25. Ibid., (italics his).

as the Egyptians were wont [i.e., accustomed]
to worship bulls, which, though not without
life, yet are destitute of that reason whereby
they would be capable of knowing the requests
of their worshippers. Others worship *devils*
instead of the true God.... These, though beings
of great powers, have not knowledge necessary
to capacitate them fully to understand the state,
circumstances, necessities, and desires of those
who pray to them.[26]

In contrast to these false gods, says Edwards, "the
true God perfectly knows the circumstances of every
one that prays to him throughout the world." Then
Edwards adds, "Though millions pray to him at once,
in different parts of the world, it is no more difficult
for him who is infinite in knowledge, to take notice of
all than of one alone."[27] In reality "God is so perfect
in knowledge, that he doth not need to be informed
by us, in order to a knowledge of our wants [i.e.,
needs]; for he knows what things we need before we
ask him."[28] On this quote Kreider comments, "These
statements seem to indicate Edwards's conviction
that God's knowledge of human decisions stands
prior to the exercise of the human will, that God's
knowledge extends to the choices that creatures have
not yet made. God's knowledge extends not only to
the entire realm of possible choices humans might

---

26. Ibid., (italics his).
27. Ibid.
28. Ibid.

make, but even extends to the actual choices they will make."[29]

D. Doctrine Defended

In the last part of his treatise,[30] Edwards defends his doctrine that God hears prayer. He does so by raising and answering two inquiries. First, why does God require us to pray in order for Him to bestow His mercy on us? Before Edwards addresses this question, he clarifies that God does not require us to pray in order that He might be informed of our petitions, for "God never gains any knowledge by information."[31] God is all knowing and His knowledge is unchangeable.[32] Edwards goes on to reason:

> He knows what we want, a thousand times more perfectly than we do ourselves, before we ask him. For though, speaking after the manner of men, God is sometimes represented as if he were moved and persuaded by the prayers of his people; yet it is not to be thought that God is properly moved or made willing by our prayers; for it is no more possible that there should be any new inclination or will in God, than new

29. Kreider, "Jonathan Edwards's Theology of Prayer," 442.

30. *The Most High, A Prayer-Hearing God* is divided into four major parts, as Edwards says: "I shall handle this point [i.e., that God hears prayer] in the following method: 1. Show that the Most High is a God *that hears prayer.* 2. That he is *eminently* such a God. 3. That herein he is *distinguished* from all false gods. 4. Give the *reasons* of the doctrine." See Ibid., 114 (italics his).

31. Ibid., 115.
32. Ibid.

knowledge. The mercy of God is not moved
or drawn by any thing in the creature; but the
spring of God's beneficence is within himself
only; he is self-moved; and whatsoever mercy
he bestows, the reason and ground of it is not to
be sought for in the creature, but in God's own
good pleasure.[33]

So why then does God require prayer in order
to bestow His mercy? Edwards gives two answers:
the one pertains to God, and the other to ourselves.
First, in relation to God,

prayer is but a sensible acknowledgement
of our dependence on him to his glory. As he
hath made all things for his own glory, so he
will be glorified and acknowledged by his creatures; and it is fit that he should require this of
those who would be the subjects of his mercy.
That we, when we desire to receive any mercy
from him, should humbly supplicate the Divine
Being for the bestowment of that mercy, is but
a suitable acknowledgment of our dependence
on the power and mercy of God for that which
we need.[34]

And second, in relation to ourselves,

God requires prayer of us in order to the
bestowment of mercy, because it tends to prepare us for its reception. Fervent prayer many
ways tends to prepare the heart.... Our prayer
to God may excite in us a suitable sense and

---

33. Ibid., 115–16.
34. Ibid., 116.

consideration of our dependence on God for the mercy we ask, and a suitable exercise of faith in God's sufficiency, that so we may be prepared to glorify his name when the mercy is received.[35]

The second question that Edwards answers as a way of contending for his doctrine is "Why is God *so ready* to hear the prayers of men?"[36] Edwards provides two replies: The first answer is that God is infinitely gracious and merciful. In other words, God hears our prayers, not because of our prayers themselves but ultimately because of His grace and mercy on us. Edwards continues, "It is indeed a very wonderful thing, that so great a God should be so ready to hear our prayers, though we are so despicable and unworthy: that he should give free access at all times to every one; should allow us to importunate without esteeming it an indecent boldness; should be so rich in mercy to them that call upon him; that worms of the dust should have such power with God by prayer."[37] Here as Edwards sees more of his misery, he sees more of God's mercy in his prayer life.

The second reply is that God is so ready to hear our prayers because "[w]e have a glorious Mediator, who has prepared the way, that our prayers may be heard consistently with the honour of God's justice and majesty." And according to Edwards this Mediator, the Lord Jesus Christ, has done three splendid

---

35. Ibid.
36. Ibid., (italics his).
37. Ibid.

things, so that our prayers may reach God's throne in heaven:

> [1] He hath by his blood made *atonement* for sin; so that our guilt need not stand in the way, as a separating wall between God and us, and that our sins might not be a cloud through which our prayers cannot pass.... [2] Christ, by his obedience, has *purchased* this privilege, viz. that the prayers of those who believe in him should be heard. He has not only removed the obstacles to our prayers, but has merited a hearing of them.... [3] Christ enforces the prayers of his people, by his *intercession* at the right hand of God in heaven.[38]

Here Edwards reveals his Christ-centered theology of prayer. Likewise, Kreider notices, "Edwards' Christocentric theology is clearly evidenced here"[39] and "forms the foundation for his theology of prayer."[40] For Edwards, coming to God without the Mediator Jesus is utterly impossible. Yes, "God would have been infinitely gracious if there had been no Mediator; but the way to the mercy-seat would have been blocked up."[41]

E. Doctrine Applied
As typical to Edwards' other sermons, *The Most High, A Prayer-Hearing God* ends with an extensive application. As a way of applying this doctrine

---

38. Ibid., (italics his).
39. Kreider, "Jonathan Edwards's Theology of Prayer," 444.
40. Ibid., 454.
41. Edwards, "The Most High, A Prayer-Hearing God," 116.

and actually concluding the message itself, Edwards reminds his audience of the great privilege they have to pray to God through Christ:

> Hence we may learn how highly we are privileged, in that we have the Most High revealed to us, who is a God that heareth prayer. The greater part of mankind are destitute of this privilege. Whatever their necessities are, whatever their calamities or sorrows, they have no prayer-hearing God to whom they may go.... How highly privileged are we, in that we have the holy word of this same God, to direct us how to seek for mercy! And whatever difficulties or distress we are in, we may go to him with confidence and great encouragement. What a comfort may this be to us! and what reason have we to rejoice in our privilege, to prize them so highly....[42]

Edwards deals with one objection that he thinks may hinder his listeners from applying this doctrine. The objection reads, "I have often prayed to God for certain mercies and he has not heard my prayers,"[43] to which Edwards replies: First, "It is no argument, that God is not a prayer-hearing God, if he give not to men *what they ask* of him to consume upon their lusts. Oftentimes when men pray for temporal good things, they desire them for no good end, but only to gratify their pride or sensuality. If they pray for worldly good things chiefly from a worldly spirit; and

---

42. Ibid., 116–17.
43. Ibid., 117.

make idol of the world; it is no wonder that God doth not hear their prayers."[44]

Second, "It is no argument that God is not a prayer-hearing God, that he heareth not *insincere* and *unbelieving* prayers."[45] Edwards asks, "How can we expect that he should have any respect to that which has no sincerity in it? God looketh not at words, but at the heart; and it is fit that he should do so [that is, not answer our hypocritical and doubting prayers]."[46]

Third, "it is no argument that he is not a prayer-hearing God, that he exercises *his own wisdom* as to the time and manner of answering prayer."[47] The seeming unanswered prayer may just mean that God's perfect time to grant that petition has not yet arrived. Edwards exhorts his audience, "The business of prayer is not to direct God, who is infinitely wise, and needs not any of our directions; who knows what is best for us ten thousand times better than we, and knows what time and what way are best. It is fit that he should answer prayer, and, as an infinitely wise God, in the exercise of his own wisdom, and not ours."[48]

Having cleared up the objection, Edwards reproves those who still find an excuse to neglect the duty and privilege of prayer. With convicting words, he declares,

---

44. Ibid., (italics his).
45. Ibid., (italics his).
46. Ibid.
47. Ibid., (italics his).
48. Ibid.

If we enjoy so great a privilege as to have the prayer-hearing God revealed to us, how great will be our folly and inexcusableness, if we neglect the privilege, or make no use of it, and deprive ourselves of the advantage by not seeking this God by prayer.... What account can those persons give of themselves, who neglect so known a duty? It is impossible that any among us should be ignorant of this command of God. How daring, therefore, is their wickedness who live in the neglect of this duty! and what can they answer to their Judge, when he shall call them to an account for it?[49]

The sermon does not end here. Edwards foresees another possible objection, which is, "If I do pray, my prayer will not be the prayer of faith [and thus will not be heard], because I am in a natural condition, and have no faith."[50] This objection came out of Edwards' previous assertion that "*God always hears the prayer* of faith."[51] Apparently those who doubt their faith in God may argue that it is pointless for them to pray since God will not listen to faithless prayer. But this reasoning, as Edwards argues, "excuses not from obedience to a plain command of God. God not only directs godly persons to pray, but others also."[52] In short, they still ought to pray on account of God's command to pray. Besides, Edwards explains:

---

49. Ibid.
50. Ibid.
51. Ibid., (italics his).
52. Ibid.

God is pleased sometimes to answer the prayers of unbelievers. Indeed he hears not their prayers for their goodness or acceptableness, or because of any true respect to him manifested in them, for there is none; nor has he obliged himself to answer such prayers; yet he is pleased sometimes, of his sovereign mercy, to pity wicked men, and hear their cries. Thus he heard the cries of the Ninevites, (Jonah iii.) and the prayer of Ahab (1 Kings xxi. 27, 28). Though there be no regard to God in their prayers, yet he, of his infinite grace, is pleased to have respect to their desires of their own happiness, and to grant their requests. He may, and sometimes does, hear the cries of wicked men, as he hears the hungry ravens, when they cry, Psal. cxlvii. 9. And he opens his bountiful hand, and satisfies the desires of every living thing, Psal. cxlv. 16. Besides the prayers of sinners, though they have no goodness in them, yet are made a means of a preparation for mercy.[53]

Finally, Edwards concludes with a brief but compelling challenge, "Seeing we have such a prayer-hearing God as we have heard, let us be much employed in the duty of prayer: let us pray with all prayer and supplication: let us live prayerful lives, continuing instant in prayer, watching thereunto with all perseverance; praying always, without ceasing, earnestly, and not fainting."[54]

---

53. Ibid.
54. Ibid.

Summary

To encapsulate Edwards' doctrine of prayer, the following points can be noted: First, his doctrine of prayer is based on a simple and yet profound truth that God hears prayer. Beck also concludes that "Edwards's theology of prayer proves to be quite simple in expression but profound in implication. Christians pray. God hears. Christians need. God supplies. Christians trust. God responds."[55] If one would ask Edwards why he prayed, the answer would probably be simply because of this basic theological fact that God hears prayer. Edwards practiced prayer because he believed God hears prayer.

Second, his doctrine of prayer is anchored in the Scripture, God the Father, and God the Son.[56] That is to say, (1) God answers prayer in agreement with His own Word. Edwards maintains that God will not listen to prayer that is "any further than he has promised in his word."[57] Thus, no one who prays outside the Bible's parameter must claim God's answer. (2) God hears prayer in harmony with His character as a merciful and gracious Father. This glorious truth, says Edwards, "is very wonderful, when we consider

---

55. Peter Beck, "The Voice of Faith: Jonathan Edwards's Theology of Prayer" (Ph.D. diss., Southern Baptist Theological Seminary, 2007), 17–18.

56. But, of course, this assertion does not mean that Edwards was anti-Trinity, and that his theology of prayer is not pneumatological. As we shall see in the next section, Edwards actually gave special emphasis to the Holy Spirit in prayer.

57. Edwards, "The Most High, A Prayer-Hearing God," 114.

the distance between God and us, and how we have
provoked him by our sins, and how unworthy we are
of the least gracious notice."[58] If God answers us it
is not really because of our prayers, but "because
God delights in mercy and condescension"[59] to pour
out His blessing upon us in response to our prayers.
(3) God hears prayer in accord with His Son, through
whom alone sinners can come to God for mercy.
Edwards teaches that "[o]ur prayers would be of no
account, and of no avail with God, were it not for the
merits of Christ."[60] Christ's "merits are the incense
that is offered with the prayers of the saints, which
render them a sweet savour to God, and acceptable
in his sight. Hence the prayers of the saints have
such power with God."[61]

Third, his doctrine of prayer is grounded in a
biblically balanced view of divine sovereignty and
human duty to pray. Though notoriously difficult to
comprehend, Edwards tries to reconcile the seeming
tension between these two. As seen in his *Personal
Narrative*, Edwards undoubtedly believes that God
is in total control of everything, and that whatever
God has decreed will surely come to pass. God is
absolutely powerful. Nonetheless, Edwards insists
that prayer "has a great power in it" in which the

---

58. Ibid., 116.
59. Ibid.
60. Ibid.
61. Ibid.

"Most High...manifests himself as conquered by it."[62] God is sovereign and yet as Edwards understood it— "God is, as it were, *overcome* by prayer."[63] God is immutable, and yet it appears in human eyes that He is moved by prayer. However, aware of the possible misconception, Edwards makes it clear:

> [T]hough, speaking after the manner of men, God is sometimes represented as if he were moved and persuaded by the prayers of his people; yet it is not to be thought that God is properly moved or made willing by our prayers; for it is no more possible that there should be any new inclination or will in God, than new knowledge. The mercy of God is not moved or drawn by any thing in the creature; but the spring of God's beneficence is within himself only; he is self-moved....[64]

In another sermon, Edwards states, "We don't cause God's ear to hear, but he causes it."[65] We do not pray to change God's mind, for His mind cannot be changed. The truth is, for Edwards, our prayer to

---

62. Ibid., 115.

63. Ibid.

64. Ibid., 116.

65. Jonathan Edwards, "God's Manner Is First to Prepare Men's Heart and Then to Answer Their Prayers," in *The Glory and Honor of God*, ed. Michael D. McMullen, vol. 2 (Nashville: Broadman & Holman Publishers, 2004), 78. Edwards adds: "The mercy of God towards his people is not moved or drawn by them but 'tis self-moved. It has its beginning, its first spring, in God himself, and the cause of it is not to be sought in the creature" (Ibid.).

God actually changes us.[66] God is omniscient; "he doth not need to be informed by us, in order to a knowledge of our wants; for he knows what things we need before we ask him." And yet Edwards strongly admonished his congregation to pray. Yes, God is sovereign, unchangeable, and all-knowing, but this does not excuse us from praying. Our duty is to pray! And as Edwards bluntly says, "They who live without prayer live like atheists or like brute creatures. They live as if there were no God, as if they had no souls and had nothing to do with God and had no need of his favor."[67] Hence, we see how Edwards sought to balance God's sovereignty and human responsibility in prayer. His argument may not satisfy his hearers, but he should be commended for his effort to address this crucial matter.

Fourth, his doctrine of prayer is focused on God's glory. Although praying is our duty, we pray ultimately for God's delight. Likewise, God hears our prayer for the primary purpose of His own glory. "Whatsoever mercy he bestows, the reason and ground of it is not to be sought for in the creature, but in God's own good pleasure," claims Edwards.[68] God glorifies Himself by answering our prayers. He "manifests himself as delighting in being sought to by prayer."[69] He delights

66. See Nichols, *Jonathan Edwards: A Guided Tour of His Life and Thoughts*, 210.

67. Edwards, "God's Manner Is First to Prepare Men's Heart and Then to Answer Their Prayers," 89.

68. Edwards, "The Most High, A Prayer-Hearing God," 116.

69. Ibid., 114.

in it because His appointed means is to shower His mercies in His providence. "God has been pleased to constitute prayer to be antecedent to the bestowment of mercy, and he is pleased to bestow mercy in consequence of prayer," Edwards writes.[70] Moreover, God delights in prayer because through it His creatures most fully acknowledge their "dependence on him to his glory."[71] Thus Beck's pronouncement is right that, for Edwards, "true prayer...focuses its attention upon God in all his magnificent glory."[72]

---

70. Cited in Nichols, *Jonathan Edwards: A Guided Tour of His Life and Thoughts* , 210.

71. Ibid., 116.

72. Beck, "The Voice of Faith: Jonathan Edwards's Theology of Prayer," 8.

CHAPTER FOUR

———— ✦ ————

Distinct Emphasis on the Holy Spirit in Prayer

In his dissertation, "The Puritan Concept and Practice of Prayer," Roy Walter Williams avouches that "experiential pneumatology" is a "unique contribution of the Puritans."[1] He further argues that "the economy of the Holy Spirit in prayer was a central concept for both the Puritan doctrine of the Christian life and the worship of the church."[2] This argument is very true for the last Puritan, Edwards, who according to Haykin "was deeply indebted to the passionate interest that seventeenth-century Puritanism had in the work of the Holy Spirit."[3] And Beck, who has done an extensive study on Edwards' theology of prayer, indicates that Edwards' pneumatic emphasis on prayer is "the most distinctive and most important part of his theology of prayer."[4]

———————————

1. Roy Walter Williams, "The Puritan Concept and Practice of Prayer" (Ph.D. diss., University of London, 1982), 81.

2. Ibid., 94.

3. Michael A.G. Haykin, *A Sweet Flame: Piety in the Letters of Jonathan Edwards* (Grand Rapids: Reformation Heritage Books, 2007), 1–2.

4. Beck said this to me in our email conversation.

The previous section highlights how Edwards' doctrine of prayer is theocentric[5] as well as Christocentric. The following section illustrates that Edwards' understanding of prayer is also very Spirit-centered, as he affirms that "our communication with God the Father and God the Son consists in our possessing of the Holy Ghost, which is their Spirit."[6] Christoph Ehrat, commenting on Edwards' affirmation, mentions that "[i]t is this divine Spirit dwelling in our hearts who takes us into the blessed, unsearchable fellowship of the Trinity."[7] Hence, Beck says, "All three Persons of the Trinity play a vital role in Edwards's theology of prayer. God expects, hears, and answers prayer. Christ mediates and facilitates prayer. The Holy Spirit motivates believers to prayer."[8]

A. The Holy Spirit as "the true spirit of prayer"

In his sermon *Hypocrites Deficient in the Duty of Prayer* (1740), Edwards rebukes those who pray hypocritically, those who neglect the duty of secret prayer. One reason he gives as to their manner is

---

5. I use this term to particularly refer to God the Father.

6. Cited in Christoph Ehrat, "Jonathan Edwards' Treatise Concerning Religious Affections and Its Application to Prayer," *Crux* 24 (1988), 15.

7. Ibid.

8. Peter Beck, "The Voice of Faith: Jonathan Edwards's Theology of Prayer" (Ph.D. diss., Southern Baptist Theological Seminary, 2007), 160.

that "[h]ypocrites never had the spirit of prayer."[9] He explains, "They may have been stirred up to the external performance of this duty, and that with a great deal of earnestness and affection, and yet always have been destitute of the true spirit of prayer."[10] For Edwards, "the true spirit of prayer is a holy spirit, a gracious spirit."[11] He further affirms, "The true spirit of prayer is no other than God's own spirit dwelling in the hearts of the saints."[12] Thus, for Edwards, the Holy Spirit is the essence of prayer without whom no one can pray. The Holy Spirit makes intercession for us. In some respects the third person of the Trinity indites our prayers or dictates us to pray, and leads us to pour out our souls before God.[13] There will be no true prayer without the Holy Spirit, for He is "the true spirit of prayer." Ehrat expresses it this way:

> As there is no true spiritual life without our being profoundly affected by the Holy Spirit, so there is no genuine prayer life without the Holy Spirit's operating in our hearts. It is God's Spirit abiding in us, not some ability that we have in ourselves, who is the source of a rich prayer life. Prayer then becomes a celebration and practice of the presence of the Holy Spirit,

9. Jonathan Edwards, "Hypocrites Deficient in the Duty of Prayer," in *The Works of Jonathan Edwards*, vol. 2, ed. Edward Hickman (1834; reprint, Edinburgh: The Banner of Truth Trust, 1974), 72.

10. Ibid.

11. Ibid.

12. Ibid.

13. Ibid.

which fundamentally differs from an approach that emphasizes techniques, postures and certain formulas.[14]

B. The Holy Spirit as "the greatest blessing that can be asked"

Edwards' pneumatological emphasis on prayer is also obvious in his sermon called *Praying for the Spirit* (1740). This sermon is based on Luke 11:13: "How much more shall your heavenly Father give the Holy Spirit to them that ask him." From this verse Edwards asseverates that "the Holy Spirit...is the greatest blessing that can be asked."[15] He is the greatest blessing because it is by Him that "we are sanctified and quickened [or made alive]." It is by Him that "we have spiritual life." It is by Him that "we are conformed to God and have his image, and have the redemption of Christ applied to us and so are possessed of all the blessings of his purchase." "In short," proclaims Edwards, it is by Him that "we are actually possessed of true holiness and happiness."[16] He is the "sum of all blessings."[17] Thus, Edwards would exhort his listeners to make the Holy Spirit

14. Ehrat, "Jonathan Edwards' Treatise Concerning Religious Affections and its Application to Prayer," 15.

15. Jonathan Edwards, "Praying for the Spirit," in *Sermons and Discourses 1739–1742*, vol. 22 of *The Works of Jonathan Edwards*, eds. Harry S. Stout, Nathan O. Hatch, and Kyle P. Farley (New Haven: Yale University Press, 2003), 214.

16. Ibid.

17. Cited in Beck, "The Voice of Faith: Jonathan Edwards's Theology of Prayer," 198.

the supreme object of their prayers, because the Holy Spirit, for Edwards, is "the sum of the blessings that Christians have to pray for."[18]

C. The Holy Spirit as "the chief subject matter of prayer"

If the Holy Spirit is the true spirit of prayer, and the greatest blessing that can be asked, then Edwards considering the Spirit of God "the chief subject matter of prayer" is no surprise.[19] The Holy Spirit is, in Beck's words, "the Alpha and Omega of prayer, the totality of all that duty entails."[20] Thus, the person as well as the work of the Spirit is central to Edwards' theology of prayer. "Let all [therefore] cry for the pouring out of the Spirit on their own souls and on others," implores Edwards.[21] Pray for the Spirit!

---

18. Cited in Ibid.

19. Jonathan Edwards, "The Suitableness of Union in Extraordinary Prayer for the Advancement of God's Church," in *Sermons and Discourses 1743–1758*, ed. Wilson H. Kimnach, vol. 25 of *The Works of Jonathan Edwards*, ed. Harry S. Stout (New Haven: Yale University Press, 2003), 203.

20. Beck, "The Voice of Faith: Jonathan Edwards's Theology of Prayer," 198.

21. Edwards, "Praying for the Spirit," 222.

CHAPTER FIVE

———— ✦ ————

Derived Lessons from
His Prayer Life

To conclude, let us answer the following question: What lessons can we glean from Edwards as a remarkable man of prayer? Before answering this question, we must realize that Edwards was a uniquely gifted person. Therefore, as Whitney says, "In one sense, it's foolish to try to imitate Edwards. He was a genius."[1] Yet, needless to say, Edwards was also a sinner like us. He had weaknesses too. Nevertheless, we can learn several lessons from him.

First, we can attempt to emulate *his devotion and discipline in prayer*. His private prayer life was indeed a reflection of this devotedly disciplined life. The fact that he was able to spend considerable time in secret prayer, despite the nature of his work as a father, pastor, teacher, and writer confirms this truth. His public persona was a result of his close commu-

---

1. Donald S. Whitney, "Pursuing A Passion For God Through Spiritual Disciplines: Learning From Jonathan Edwards," in *A God Entranced Vision of All Things: The Legacy of Jonathan Edwards*, eds. John Piper and Justin Taylor (Wheaton: Crossway Books, 2004), 125.

nion with God. If he was a great theologian, it was because he spent a great amount of time in prayer. Consequently, he could preach, by God's grace, with all boldness and clear conscience against those hypocrites who shrugged off the duty of secret prayer. He was not hesitant to do so because he practiced what he preached.

Another example that we can follow from his life is *his delight in the three persons of God in prayer.* The triune God was so dear to him. Edwards loved God, and so he enjoyed talking to his Lord. He prayed not only to ask a gift, but also to give God glory. He used prayer as a means of not only pleading for God's mercy, but also praising God for such mercy. Prayer, for Edwards, is an act of praise and worship.

Lastly, we must not forget that his deep devotion and delight in prayer was a fruit of *his diligence in his study of the Scripture.* Prayer and God's Word are inseparable for Edwards. He knew that growing in prayer apart from a proper knowledge of the Holy Word is impossible. He bled the Bible, so to speak, to get the true blood of prayer, and this blood was flowing into his spiritual vein. Thus, as this blood flowed naturally into his vein, so did his prayer from his mind and heart. He could therefore say by God's grace: "Prayer seemed to be natural to me, as a breath by which the inward burnings of my heart had vent."[2]

2. Cited in Sereno E. Dwight, "Memoirs of Jonathan Edwards," in *The Works of Jonathan Edwards*, vol. 1, ed Edward Hickman (1834; reprint, Edinburgh: Banner of Truth Trust, 1974), xiii.

Annotated Bibliography

Bakke, Robert Oscar. "The Concert of Prayer: Back to the Future?" D.Min. diss., Gordon-Conwell Theological Seminary, 1993.

   In this dissertation, Bakke examines an important aspect of Jonathan Edwards' theology of prayer, namely, the concert of prayer. In his examination Bakke focuses on Edwards' treatise, titled heavily, *An Humble Attempt to Promote Explicit Agreement and Visible Union of God's People in Extraordinary Prayer, for the Revival of Religion and Advancement of Christ's Kingdom on Earth* (1748). Edwards' purpose in this treatise is well explained by the title.

Beck, Peter. "The Voice of Faith: Jonathan Edwards's Theology of Prayer." Ph.D. diss., Southern Baptist Theological Seminary, 2007.

   This masterful dissertation thoroughly analyzes Edwards' theology of prayer. It has convincingly proven that Edwards deserves to be called the theologian of prayer.

Brand, David C. *Profile of the Last Puritan: Jonathan Edwards, Self-Love, and the Dawn of the Beatific.* Atlanta, Ga.: Scholars Press, 1991.

   Some historians do not consider Edwards a Puritan. In his book, however, Brand calls Edwards the last Puritan. Brand studies the life and thought of this last Puritan with a special attention to his views on self-love.

Edwards, Jonathan. *The Works of Jonathan Edwards.* 2 vols. Edited by Edward Hickman. Edinburgh: Banner of Truth Trust, 1974.

This two-volume set contains four important discourses on prayer: (1) "Hypocrites Deficient in the Duty of Prayer," (2) "An Humble Attempt to Promote Explicit Agreement and Visible Union of God's People in Extraordinary Prayer, for the Revival of Religion and Advancement of Christ's Kingdom on Earth," (3) "The Most High, A Prayer-Hearing God," and (4) "Hypocrites Deficient in the Duty of Prayer." The set also includes Sereno E. Dwight's *Memoirs of Jonathan Edwards.*

———. *Letters and Personal Writings.* Vol. 16 of *The Works of Jonathan Edwards.* Edited by George S. Claghorn. New Haven: Yale University Press, 1998.

This scholarly volume incorporates Edwards' "Resolutions," "Diary," and "Personal Narrative." In his introduction to "Diary," Claghorn says: "The 'Diary' also tells much about his attitude toward prayer. Personal communion with the Almighty, which was to be a hallmark of his theology, was an experience Edwards sought on a daily basis. As in the 'Personal Narrative,' he mentions singing during devotion a number of times. Several brief prayers are included in the 'Diary,' with reminders of the need for prayer, along with instructions on the proper method of praying."

———. *A Call to United, Extraordinary Prayer.* Introduced by David Bryant. Ross-shire, U.K.: Christian Heritage, 2003.

This book was originally published in 1748 under the long title *An Humble Attempt to Promote Explicit Agreement and Visible Union of God's People in Extraordinary Prayer, for the Revival of Religion and Advancement of Christ's Kingdom on Earth*. The 2003 edition has a helpful introduction that explains why Edwards wrote his treatise and why this antique treatise is still relevant today.

―――. *Sermons and Discourses 1739–1742*. Vol. 22 of *The Works of Jonathan Edwards*. Edited by Harry S. Stout, Nathan O. Hatch, and Kyle P. Farley. New Haven: Yale University Press, 2003.

When looking for sermons preached by Edwards during the years 1739–1742, this volume is an outstanding reference. One of the sermons in this volume is "Praying for the Spirit," which was delivered in 1740 and was based on Luke 11:13. This sermon has contributed to my study of Edwards' view of the Holy Spirit in relation to prayer.

―――. *Sermons and Discourses 1743–1758*. Vol. 25 of *The Works of Jonathan Edwards*. Edited by Wilson H. Kimnach. New Haven: Yale University Press, 2003.

This work includes Edwards' sermon on Zechariah 8:20–22. The sermon is titled "The Suitableness of Union in Extraordinary Prayer for the Advancement of God's Church," in which the preacher calls his congregation to unite in prayer for the progress of God's work in this world. The message underscores the concept of concerted prayer, an emphasis present also in Edwards' treatise *An Humble Attempt* (1748).

―――. *Praying Together for True Revival*. Edited by T. M. Moore. Phillipsburg: Presbyterian & Reformed Publishing, 2004.

Moore's edition makes Edwards' classic work

An Humble Attempt (1748) accessible to a modern audience. This 2004 edition also contains a valuable introduction by John H. Armstrong to Edwards' work. I have only cited this book to alert my readers about this introduction.

―――. *Glory and Honor of God*. Vol. 2. Edited by Michael D. McMullen. Nashville: Broadman & Holman Publishers, 2004.

Readers will profit from this collection of Edwards' previously unpublished sermons. One of the messages in this volume is "God's Manner Is First to Prepare Men's Heart and Then to Answer Their Prayers." Delivered in 1735, this sermon is an exposition of Psalm 10:17 in which Edwards explains the elements of true prayer.

Ehrat, Christoph. "Jonathan Edwards' Treatise Concerning Religious Affections and Its Application to Prayer." *Crux* 24 (1988): 11–16.

This brief article provides a summary of Edwards' famous discourse *Religious Affections* (1746). It also shows how Edwards' twelve signs of true spiritual conversion in his discourse relate to genuine prayer.

The Golden Treasury of Puritan Quotations. Compiled and Edited by Isaac David Ellis Thomas. Carlisle, Pa.: Banner of Truth Trust, 1977.

Arranged alphabetically and topically, this collection of quotations from the sixteenth- and seventeenth-century Puritans is a handy tool for writers and speakers. It has quotations on prayer, but since it focuses on sixteenth- and seventeenth-century Puritanism, no quotation is by Edwards. Nonetheless, I have found a quotation here that helps me illustrate Edwards' view on prayer.

Haykin, Michael A. G. *Jonathan Edwards: The Holy Spirit in Revival*. Darlington, Co. Durham/Webster, NY: Evangelical Press, 2005.

    Haykin's book has a chapter called "The Humble Attempt and Praying for Revival." This section exposes readers to Edwards' view of prayer, especially the concert of prayer in conjunction with revival.

————. *A Sweet Flame: Piety in the Letters of Jonathan Edwards*. Grand Rapids: Reformation Heritage Books, 2007.

    This book, a part of the Profiles in Reformed Spirituality series, is a collection of Edwards' letters edited and annotated by Haykin. The volume also includes a biographical introduction to Edwards' spirituality.

Kreider, Glenn R. "Jonathan Edwards's Theology of Prayer," *Bibliotheca Sacra* 160, no. 640 (2003): 434–56.

    In light of Edwards' sermon *The Most High, A Prayer-Hearing God*, Kreider investigates Edwards' theology of prayer. Preached in 1736, this sermon was derived from Psalm 65:2, "O thou that hearest prayer." I have relied heavily on Kreider's investigation for my own study of Edwards' sermon.

Marsden, George M. *Jonathan Edwards: A Life*. New Haven: Yale University Press, 2003.

    This massive volume is regarded as the definitive biography of Edwards. Written in chronological sequence, the book presents more of Edwards' mind than his heart.

Murray, Iain H. *Jonathan Edwards: A New Biography*. Edinburg: Banner of Truth Trust, 1996.

    A standard biography of Edwards, this work highlights more of Edwards' spirituality than his theology.

Thus Murray's biography is a superb companion to Marsden's.

Nichols, Stephen. *Jonathan Edwards: A Guided Tour of His Life and Thought*. Philipsburg: Presbyterian & Reformed Publishing, 2001.

A blend of biography, history, and theology, this book explores Edwards' life and thoughts. Those who are new to Edwards may want to start with this book.

Williams, Roy Walter. "The Puritan Concept and Practice of Prayer," Ph.D. diss., University of London, 1982.

This dissertation is a great contribution to the study of Puritanism, especially with regard to the subject of private, family, and public prayer.

Whitney, Donald S. "Pursuing A Passion For God Through Spiritual Disciplines: Learning From Jonathan Edwards," in *A God Entranced Vision of All Things: The Legacy of Jonathan Edwards*. Edited by John Piper and Justin Taylor. Wheaton: Crossway Books, 2004.

This chapter does what its title states. Using Edwards as an example, Whitney carefully helps his readers pursue a love for God through spiritual disciplines.

———— ✦ ————

Prayers and Prayer Requests by Jonathan Edwards

Letter to George Whitefield

Writing from Northampton, Massachusetts on December 14, 1740, Jonathan Edwards told his fellow preacher of the gospel, George Whitefield (1714–1770), about the revival at Northampton and asked him to pray for him. Edwards' prayer request is noteworthy:

Northampton, December 14, 1740

Rev. and Dear Sir,

I have joyful tidings to send you concerning the state of religion in this place. It has been gradually reviving and prevailing more and more, ever since you [were] here. Religion [becomes] abundantly more the subject of conversation; other things that seemed to impede it, are for the present laid aside. I have reason to think that a considerable number of our young people, some of them children, have already been savingly brought home to Christ. I hope salvation has come to this house since you [were] in it, with respect to one, if not more, of my children. The Spirit of God seems to be at work with others of the family. That blessed work seems now to be going on in this place, especially amongst those that are young.

And as God seems to have succeeded your labors amongst us, and prayers for us, I desire your fervent prayers for us may yet be continued, that God would not be to us as a wayfaring man, that turns aside to tarry but for a night, but that he would more and more pour out his Spirit upon us, and no more depart from us; and for me in particular, that I may be filled with his Spirit, and may become fervent, as a flame of fire in my work, and may be abundantly succeeded, and that it would please God, however unworthy I am, to improve me as an instrument of his glory, and advancing the kingdom of Christ.

[Jonathan Edwards.][1]

---

1. Jonathan Edwards, "Letter to the Reverend George Whitefield," in *Letters and Personal Writings*, ed. George S. Claghorn, vol. 16 of *The Works of Jonathan Edwards*, ed. Harry S. Stout (New Haven: Yale University Press, 1998), 87.

Letter to Joseph Bellamy

One of the students of Jonathan Edwards was Joseph Bellamy (1719–1790). Born in Connecticut, Bellamy became an important preacher, New Divinity theologian, and writer of his time. In Edwards' letter to Bellamy dated January 21, 1741/2, Edwards urges him to pray for the recurrence of revival at Northampton, Massachusetts. Here is an excerpt from the letter:

Northampton, January 21, 1741/2

Rev. and Dear Sir,

Religion in this and the neighboring towns has now of late been on the decaying hand. I desire your prayers that God would quicken and revive us again, and particularly that he would greatly humble, and pardon, and quicken me; and fill me with his own fullness; and, if it may consist with his will, improve me as an instrument to revive his work. There has been the year past the most wonderful work amongst children here, by far, that ever was: God has seemed almost wholly to take a new generation, that are come on since the late great work seven years ago.

I pray that Christ our good shepherd will be with you and direct you and greatly strengthen and bless you....

I am, dear Sir, your affectionate and unworthy

Brother and fellow-laborer,
Jonathan Edwards.[2]

---

2. Edwards, "Letter to the Reverend Joseph Bellamy," in *Letters and Personal Writings*, 98–100.

Letter to daughter, Mary Edwards

Jonathan Edwards and his wife, Sarah Pierpont (1710–1758), had eleven children (three sons and eight daughters). One of their daughters was Mary Edwards (1734–1807) who became the wife of Timothy Dwight Jr. (1726–1777). When Mary was fifteen years old and was in Portsmouth, New Hampshire, Jonathan Edwards wrote her a letter in which he expressed his daily prayer for her.

Northampton, July 26, 1749

Dear Child,

You may well think that it is natural for a parent to be concerned for a child at so great a distance, so far out of view, and so far out of the reach of communication; where, if you should be taken with any dangerous sickness that should issue in death, you might probably be in your grave before we could hear of your danger.

But yet my greatest concern is for your soul's good. Though you are at so great a distance from us, yet God is everywhere. You are much out of the reach of our care, but you are every moment in his hands. We have not the comfort of seeing you, but he sees you. His eye is always upon you. And if you may but be sensibly nigh to him, and have his gracious presence, 'tis no matter though you are far distant from us. I had rather you should remain hundreds of miles distant from us and have God nigh to you by his Spirit, than to have you always with us, and live at a distance from God....

My desire and daily prayer is that you may, if it may consist with the holy will of God, meet with God where you be, and have much of his divine influences on your heart wherever you may be, and that in God's due time you may be returned to us again in all respects under the smiles of heaven, and especially in prosperous circumstances in your soul; and that you may find all us alive....

I hope you will maintain a strict and constant watch over yourself and against all temptations: that you don't forget and forsake God; and particularly that you don't grow slack in secret religion. Retire often from this vain world, and all its bubbles, empty shadows, and vain amusements, and converse with God alone; and seek that divine grace and comfort, the least drop of which is more worth than all the riches, gaiety, pleasures and entertainments of the whole world....

...the whole family has indeed much to put us in mind and make us sensible of our dependence on God's care and kindness, and of the vanity of all human dependences. And we are very loudly called to seek his face, trust in him, and walk closely with him. Commending you to the care and special favor of an heavenly Father, I am

> Your very affectionate father,
> Jonathan Edwards.

Your mother and all the family give their love to you.[3]

---

3. Edwards, "Letter to Mary Edwards," in *Letters and Personal Writings*, 288–90.

Letter to son, Timothy Edwards

Jonathan Edwards had a son, Timothy Edwards (1738–1813), who left home to study at the College of New Jersey (now called Princeton University). While in Newark, New Jersey, Timothy became severely sick. To comfort his son, who at that time was only fourteen years old, Jonathan Edwards sent him a letter from Stockbridge, Massachusetts. In this letter Edwards offers a word of prayer for his son and reminds his son of his own duty to pray to God for mercy. Here is an extract from the letter:

Stockbridge, April 1, 1753

My Dear Child,

Before you will receive this letter, the matter will doubtless be determined, as to your having the smallpox. You will either be sick with that distemper, or will be past danger of having it, from any infection taken in your voyage. But whether you are sick or well, like to die or like to live, I hope you are earnestly seeking your salvation....

Till you have savingly believed in Christ, all your desires, and pains, and prayers lay God under no obligation; and if they were ten thousand times as great as they are, you must still know, that you would be in the hands of a sovereign God, who hath mercy on whom he will have mercy. Indeed, God often hears the poor, miserable cries of sinful, vile creatures, who have no manner of true regard to him in their hearts; for he is a God of infinite mercy and he delights to show mercy for his Son's sake; who is worthy, though you are unworthy; who came to save the sinful and the miserable, some of the chief of sinners.

Therefore, there is your only hope; and in him must be your refuge, who invites you to come to him, and says, "He that cometh to me, I will in no wise cast out" [John 6:37]. Whatever your circumstances are, it is your duty not to despair, but to hope in infinite mercy through a Redeemer. For God makes it your duty to pray to him for mercy which would not be your duty, if it was allowable for you to despair. We are expressly commanded to call upon God in the day of trouble; and when we are afflicted, then to pray.

I earnestly desire, that God would make you wise to salvation and that he would be merciful and gracious to you in every respect, according as he knows your circumstances require. And this is the daily prayer of

> Your affectionate and tender father,
> Jonathan Edwards.

P.S. Your mother and all the family send their love to you, as being tenderly concerned for you.[4]

---

4. "Letter to Timothy Edwards," in *Letters and Personal Writings*, 578–80.

Sermon Conclusion at
David Brainerd's Funeral

When Jonathan Edwards wrote his biography of David Brainerd (1718–1747), he entitled it "An Account of the Life of the Late Reverend Mr. David Brainerd, Minister of the Gospel, Missionary to the Indians [Native Americans], from the Honourable Society in Scotland, for the Propagation of Christian Knowledge, and Pastor of A Church of Christian Indians in New Jersey...." This long title briefly describes Brainerd, a faithful and diligent servant of Jesus Christ. At the young age of twenty-nine, Brainerd died from tuberculosis in Edwards' house. According to Edwards, a few days before Brainerd died, "though he was then so low that he could scarcely speak, he so exerted himself that he made a prayer very audibly, wherein besides praying for those present and for his own congregation, he earnestly prayed for the reviving and flourishing of religion in the world."[5] At the funeral of Brainerd, Edwards delivered a sermon which ended with the following prayerful words:

> Oh, that the things that were seen and heard in this extraordinary person, his holiness, heavenliness, labor and self-denial in life, his so remarkable devoting himself and his all, in

5. Jonathan Edwards, "A Sermon Preached on the Day of the Funeral of the Rev. Mr. David Brainerd," in *The Life of David Brainerd*, ed. Norman Pettit, vol. 7 of *The Works of Jonathan Edwards*, ed. John E. Smith (New Haven: Yale University Press, 1985), 551.

heart and practice, to the glory of God, and the wonderful frame of mind manifested, in so steadfast a manner, under the expectation of death, and the pains and agonies that brought it on, may excite in us all, both ministers and people, a due sense of the greatness of the work we have to do in the world, the excellency and amiableness of thorough religion in experience and practice, and the blessedness of the end of such whose death finishes such a life, and the infinite value of their eternal reward, when absent from the body and present with the Lord; and effectually stir us up to endeavors that in the way of such an holy life we may at last come to so blessed an end. Amen![6]

---

6. Ibid., 553–54.

—— ✦ ——

"The Sister of my heart":
Esther Edwards Burr on Faithful Friendship[1]

On October 11, 1754, Esther Edwards Burr (1732–58), the third of Jonathan and Sarah Pierpont Edwards' eleven children, writing in her diary, called her best friend Sarah Prince (1728–1771): "the Sister of my heart." The special spiritual friendship between these two godly young women is largely recorded in Esther's *Journal* written between 1754 and 1757. According to Roger Lundin and Mark Noll, this *Journal* "shows us a very busy young mother who yet took time, amid her pressing duties, to reflect on her relationship with God. The life that shines forth in the diary is one of sincere religion, hard work, family joys and sorrows, nearly overwhelming domestic responsibility, and faithful friendship."[2] This faithful friendship is the focus of this brief article.

---

1. This appendix, with very slight changes, has previously appeared in *Banner of Sovereign Grace Truth* 18, no. 10 (2010): 282–83. Used by permission.

2. Roger Lundin and Mark A. Noll, *Voices from the Heart: Four Centuries of American Piety* (Grand Rapids: William B. Eerdmans Publishing Co., 1987), 100.

Esther was accustomed to change. When her father was discharged from his congregation in Northampton over the issue of the Lord's Supper, her family was forced to leave Northampton for Stockbridge in 1752, shortly before she married.[3] In 1752, at the age of twenty, Esther married Aaron Burr, Sr. (1716–1757), a pious Presbyterian pastor and the second President of the College of New Jersey, located in Newark, New Jersey.[4] In 1756, the same year Esther bore her second and last child, Aaron Jr., who would later become the second Vice-President of the United States, the College moved to Princeton and became known as Princeton University.[5] Esther eventually relocated from Newark to Princeton, where she died in 1758 at the age of only twenty six.

While living in Newark, Esther, although happily married to Aaron, often experienced homesickness caused by her separation from her beloved family and friends. Because her husband's ministerial and administrative work load kept him in the church and school, she spent much of her day lonely at home. Finding new friends was difficult for her, especially

3. See Introduction to *The Journal of Esther Edwards Burr 1754–1757*, eds. Carol F. Karlsen and Laurie Crumpacker, (1984; repr., Eugene, Orlando: Wipf and Stock Publishers, 2010), 13.

4. According to Lundin and Noll, Esther married in 1750 at the age of eighteen. See *Voices from the Heart: Four Centuries of American Piety*, 100. I follow the date given by Gerald R. McDermott, "Burr, Esther Edwards," in *Dictionary of Evangelical Biography 1730–1860*, vol. 1, ed. Donald M. Lewis (Oxford: Blackwell Publishers, 1995), 175.

5. Esther gave birth to her first child, Sally, in 1754.

since the "wives of her husband's associates tended to be considerably older than she."[6] Thus her old-time friendship with Sarah Prince, although long-distance, became a constant source of comfort. Two years after marriage, while she and her husband were still in Newark, Esther wrote to Sarah Prince in Boston:

> It is a great comfort to me when my friends are absent from me that I have 'em some where in the World, and you my dear for one, not of the least, for I esteem you one of the best, and in some respects nerer than any Sister I have. I have not one Sister I can write so freely to as to you the Sister of my heart. There is a friend nerer than a Brother, sertainly.... That old proverb is not a true one, out of sight out of mind.[7]

Esther and Sarah had been acquainted with each other from early girlhood. In fact, Sarah's father, Thomas Prince, a Congregational pastor in Boston, was a friend of Jonathan Edwards and a leading supporter of the Great Awakening.[8] It is important to note that the Evangelical Revival of the 1730s and 1740s coincided with Esther's formative years, and, by the time she became a teenager, she expe-

---

6. Introduction to *The Journal of Esther Edwards Burr 1754–1757*, eds. Karlsen and Crumpacker, 15.

7. *The Journal of Esther Edwards Burr 1754–1757*, eds. Karlsen and Crumpacker, 53.

8. For a very short biography of Thomas Prince, see Christopher Grasso, "Prince, Thomas," in *Dictionary of Evangelical Biography 1730–1860*, vol. 2, ed. Donald M. Lewis (Oxford: Blackwell Publishers, 1995), 904–5.

rienced gospel conversion under the ministry of her father.[9] As she grew up and matured spiritually, her piety became increasingly evident. One important area of her life in which this piety manifests itself is in her friendship with Sarah, which began early in their childhood.

Esther's move to Newark made regular communication with Sarah in Boston a challenge. However, in 1754, Sarah visited Esther. What a joyous time the reunion was for the two! It "was probably at this time that they decided to maintain their intimacy by keeping journals for one another."[10] Their main purpose for exchanging journals was to keep an eye on each other's spiritual life in Christ. They did not use these journals to gossip or talk nonsense, but to talk about religion. As Esther says in her letter to Sarah written on April 20, 1755:

> I feel thankfull that you are so *blessed*—Tis not fit that I should have everything agreeable. I have already a *Thousand, Thousand*, more mercies than I make a good improvement of—I esteem *religious Conversation* one of the best helps to keep up religion in the soul, excepting *secret devotion*, I dont know but the very best—Then what a lamentable thing that tis so neglected by God's own Children."[11]

---

9. Introduction to *The Journal of Esther Edwards Burr 1754–1757*, eds. Karlsen and Crumpacker, 12.

10. Ibid., 15.

11. *The Journal of Esther Edwards Burr 1754–1757*, eds. Karlsen and Crumpacker, 112.

In this sense, Esther and Sarah were like the Puritans who regarded journaling as a means of sanctifying grace. And since their journaling was done in the context of their friendship, they no doubt also viewed their friendship as a means to grow in holiness.

Esther and Sarah both took their friendship very seriously. In her letter to Sarah dated October 5, 1754, Esther explains that to not keep a vow in friendship is sin: "I call it sin, for I look on the ties of Friendship as *sacred* and I am of your mind, that it aught to be [a] matter of Solemn Prayer to God (where there is a friendship contracted) that it may be preserved. And it is what I have done and shall continue to do."[12] This quote demonstrates Esther's high and holy view of friendship. Such view is rarely seen today even among Christian friends. In this present generation, few are like Esther and Sarah who considered friendship sacred. Certainly, the friendship of the two was not without trials, but by God's grace, the two remained loyal friends until death. This is faithful friendship!

Let us ask ourselves: Are we faithful friends? What kind of friends do we have? Do our friends help us become more like Christ? And finally, how do we view our friendship with others? Do we view friendship as a means to grow in holiness?

---

12. Ibid., 51–52.

—— ✦ ——

A Prayer for the New Year
(adapted from Jonathan Edwards' Resolutions)[1]

Lord God Almighty,
I understand that I am unable
to do anything without your help,
so I ask you to enable me
by your grace to fulfill your will.

Give me grace to do whatever
brings most glory and honor to you,
pleasure and profit to me,
and life and love to others.

Help me to number my days,
spending my time wisely,
living my life with all my might
while I still have breath.

---

1. This prayer, drawn from the first twenty one resolutions of Edwards, is by Trevin Wax; accessed 23 November 2012; available from: http://thegospelcoalition.org/blogs/trevinwax/2010/01/03/a-prayer-for-the-new-year-adapted-from-jonathan-edwards-resolutions/; Internet.

Humble me in the knowledge
that I am chief of sinners;
when I hear of the sins of others,
help me to not look upon them with pride,
but to look upon myself with shame,
confessing my own sins to you.

When I go through difficulties and trials,
remind me of the pains of hell
from which you have already delivered me.

Place people in my path who need my help,
and give me a compassionate and generous spirit.

Fill my heart with such love
that I would never do anything
out of a spirit of revenge,
nor lose my temper with those around me.
Hold my tongue when I am tempted
to speak evil of others.

Thank you for the gospel and for the hope of glory.
Help me to live in light of these
truths every day of my life,
so that when the time of my death arrives,
I will rest assuredly in you,
and you will be most glorified in me.

In Christ's name...

ABOUT THE AUTHOR

Born and reared in the Philippines, Brian G. Najapfour has been a minister of God since 2001. Called to the gospel ministry at the young age of sixteen, he began his theological education in 1997 at the Center for Biblical Studies Institute and Seminary in the Philippines. There, with God's help, he earned his Bachelor of Theology (B.Th.) degree in 2001, followed by his Master in Biblical Studies (M.B.S.) degree in 2004. From 2001 until his coming to the U.S. in 2006, he served as a pastor in the Philippines. With a desire to further his education, however, he arrived in Grand Rapids, Michigan in 2006, where he enrolled in Puritan Reformed Theological Seminary. There, he studied for his Master of Theology (Th.M.) degree, which he completed by God's grace in 2009.

While pursuing a Ph.D. degree, Najapfour, since his installation on October 19, 2012, has been pastor of Dutton United Reformed Church, Caledonia, Michigan. He is co-editor (along with Joel R. Beeke) of *Taking Hold of God: Reformed and Puritan Perspectives on Prayer* (2011) and author of *The Very Heart of Prayer: Reclaiming John Bunyan's Spirituality* (2012) and *Child Dedication: Considered Historically, Theologically, and Pastorally* (2014).

He and his wife Sarah, have three children, Anna, James, and Abigail. For more information about him, visit his website: biblicalspiritualitypress.org.

Printed in Great Britain
by Amazon

29492432R00050